I do know some people who, even though they're no longer working and so have no need to hide their breath, still choose vodka martinis instead of gin martinis. What they say is, "Gin doesn't agree with me." What they really mean is, they can no longer handle a gin martini. Somehow, there's just nothing with more authority. And I, for one, deplore its passing.

CHAPTER SIX

Spending Money in Your Golden Years

Spending money on a custom-made shirt

ONE OF THE AMAZING THINGS I've found out about being retired is that I have more money to spend now than I ever had before. And not much of anything worthwhile to spend it on. I've worked hard all my life at a good job, I've saved my money for the Golden Years, and now I'm in them! But I don't want anything. So I just keep on saving, and I hate it.

I can't even remember the things I used to want, the things that I put off until the Golden Years.

It's amazing how the cost of living goes down as you grow

older. Of course, the children are all grown and gone and off the payroll, so that's a big economy. The house is paid for. Not only that, but I could sell it for a whole lot more than I paid for it. Everything else is paid for, too, long ago.

When we were younger, we used to spend a lot more money on food than we do now. Nowadays, all we ever eat is fish and lettuce with an occasional side of cottage cheese. My wife used to make things like cherries jubilee and baked Alaska, can you believe it! But any more it's just fish and lettuce. I used to maintain a well-stocked bar with fancy expensive brands to set out. Nowadays I've learned that there's no point to pay extra for those expensive brands. In fact, if I set out expensive brands, my friends would think I'd lost my mind. They all know it's nuts to pay extra to show off those high-priced labels. We didn't know that when we were younger. Last Christmas somebody gave me one of those super-expensive bottles of Scotch that come in a metal box and so forth, and do you know, I still have that whole thing. I'll have to give it to somebody for Christmas.

Fancy cars are one way that a lot of people like to spend money. I've been a little deprived in this area because for years my company has leased a car for me to drive. I've had a new car every three years, and it's been a perfectly acceptable big, shiny new car, a Ford. Not a BMW or anything like that, but perfectly acceptable. Now that I've retired, the lease on my last Ford has run out, so I've got to go buy myself a car.

I said to my wife, "Now, after all these years, I'm going to buy myself a BMW!"

She said, "Look it over first. I don't think you'll like it."

I looked it over and I didn't like it. I looked at some other cars, too, a Saab and a Porsche. I didn't like them either.

My wife said, "Why don't you buy a Ford? You know where the buttons are on a Ford, and you're too old to change." So I bought a new Ford. It was identical to the old one, but I know where all the buttons are.

Other ways that people like to spend their money is to take trips. We do that sometimes, and I will say for it that it's expensive; traveling has that much going for it, at least. But you can't be taking trips all the time. I was looking for something out in the messy garage the other day and my wife said, "If I ever stay home long enough to get the time, we can clean out this garage." This is her way of telling me that we've been taking too many trips.

Also, on the last couple of trips we've taken, I've come home sick. I don't blame this on exotic foreign food or anything like that, but just on traveling in general. Every time we come home, and sometimes we're both sick for a few weeks afterward, my wife says, "Well, that's enough traveling for the time being."

We're going to continue taking trips, however, only maybe not quite so often. And certainly not until the garage is cleaned up.

But the other day something happened that made me sit up and take notice. My wife asked our daughter what our son-in-law would like for his birthday, and our daughter said her husband could use a new shirt. My wife asked what size and so forth, and our daughter said, "Oh, he gets his shirts custom made. You don't need to know his size, they know it."

I overheard this because I was sitting around the house with nothing much to do except make another deposit in my savings account, and my ears really perked up.

I thought to myself, "This lad is no dummy! What a really great way to spend money. I'll go order some custom shirts for myself." I have noticed for a few years that the regular $19.95 Arrow shirts which my wife buys for me don't seem to fit quite as well as they used to. They're either skimping on the cloth or they've changed the design or something, because they're too tight at the neck and around the waist. So some custom-made shirts would definitely be in order.

I found the custom-made shirt place and went in for a

fitting. There was this nice young fellow all dressed up in a custom-made shirt, and he measured me up and down and sideways and showed me all the different fabrics and colors I could order.

You know what those custom-made shirts cost? I couldn't believe it! Fifty dollars apiece! I would have two and a half new Arrow shirts for that price or maybe even three if my wife waited until they were on sale.

But I ordered four of them anyway, after I got over the heart attack I was having right there in the store. And you know how long it takes to get them? Three months! You have to wait three months for four shirts. It's a good thing I hadn't thrown away all those old Arrow shirts. You don't buy custom-made shirts in an emergency, that's for sure.

So, a while ago the young fellow who measured me called up and said my shirts were ready. The three months just flew by, and I'd forgotten all about having ordered them. So I went down and picked them up two or three weeks ago and put them on the shelf in my closet. Since then we haven't gone anywhere nice enough to warrant wearing a custom-made shirt. I don't go to the office any more, of course, and I can't cut the grass in a custom-made shirt. Nowadays when we go to church we go to an "informal" service which is held outside on the lawn, where they play Peter, Paul and Mary songs on the guitar, and everybody dresses "comfortably," which means it's no place for a new custom-made shirt.

But I've got them now, and I'll wear them sometime, and I hope they fit, because it would be fun to call up that store and order more of the same over the telephone. That's what my son-in-law does, and I think it's terrific.

Buying other new clothes for myself is another really great way to spend money fast, and I did that the other day, too. I bought a new tuxedo, for one thing. I've been wearing the same old tuxedo for probably twenty years, and while that doesn't mean I've actually worn it for very many hours, it does mean that my figure has changed a little since it was fitted to me. The last time I wore it, I split the seat, which I had already done a couple of times before, and this time my wife said she couldn't fix it.

The new one was a terribly expensive suit, and I really hated to buy it because the style in tuxedos hasn't changed. The new one looks exactly like the old one. In fact, just the other night I had to dress up in my tuxedo, and I got out the old one by mistake and didn't realize I didn't have any seat in my pants until I was already at the party.

All my life I've been buying my clothes at a store where they have all these gentlemanly-looking salesmen standing around who never, ever, notice me. I walk in, and there's no other customers there, but the salesmen just keep on with their earnest conversation in the corner. I stand around for a while and then eventually walk out and come back another day when they're not so busy.

I've always thought they were saving themselves for their big-deal customers, the older, affluent, portly gentlemen who come in and buy six-hundred-dollar suits by the dozen. Now, however, I fall into that category: I'm older, affluent and portly. But they still don't pay any attention to me when I walk into the store.

But this particular store has modernized a little bit, and now they have an attractive young lady in that department, and I'll say that she pays attention to me! In fact, I spent the afternoon with her there the other day, and I spent so much money it made my eyes bug out when I got the bill.

Now we're going to have to go some place really nice, where I can wear my four new custom-made shirts and my three new suits while they all still fit me.

CHAPTER SEVEN

A Lakeside Retreat

Big excitement for the Golden Years

ONE THING YOU OUGHT TO HAVE if you're thinking about retiring is a lakeside retreat. Or a seaside retreat or a mountainside retreat or a desert retreat or something like that, depending on what's available in the way of retreats in your part of the country.

Where I live the big thing is lakeside retreats, and I'm very glad we have one.

It's not anything at all like what you might think. I mean, it's a really old "fishin' shack." Nowadays everybody's got themselves a lovely suburban-type home at the lake with wall-to-wall carpeting and built-in stereo and built-in Hoover system and so on. But we've had our lake house for a good many years, long before it was a fancy thing to do. But it's perfectly adequate and, as I say, I'm very glad we have it because, being retired, it's the perfect place to go when you don't have anything else to do, which is a good part of the time.

It's a three-hour drive from our house in the city. That's absolutely the perfect driving time. It's a long enough trip so you know you've gone somewhere, but not long enough to make you get homesick which I have a tendency to do when I'm further away than that from home.

Years ago, when our children were young and we had this same old fishin' cabin as a lakeside retreat, my wife and I would pile the kids into the car on a Friday evening and drive like mad for three hours. Then we'd spend the weekend enjoying ourselves and our kids and the lake and getting poison ivy and so forth, and have a really good time.

Nowadays, of course, I'm pretty much retired, and most of our children have moved away to some place else, but we still have the fishin' cabin and we still spend some time there. Now, however, we pack up the dog and the cat instead of the kids and take them to the lake. In a way, it's better than it used to be, because the dog and the cat can't bring their friends with them, and they can't complain the whole time they're at the lake, and if they get poison ivy, we never know it.

Sometimes I'm sitting around at our house in the city not doing much of anything because I'm pretty much retired and I don't play golf or anything time-consuming like that, and I say, "Let's pack up the dog and the cat and go to the lake."

Most of the time, my wife says, "Great. We'll go tomorrow right after my piano lesson, and we can stay until Thursday afternoon when I have my hair appointment." Those seem to me like fairly inconsequential anchors on which to build your life, but at least there is time in between them to go to the lakeside retreat for a few days. So we go.

One thing I forgot to mention about packing up the dog and the cat is that when I say, "Let's go to the lake," they both understand it. The dog goes out and gets in the car, but the cat goes into hiding somewhere in the house, and the toughest thing about packing for the lake is finding the cat. The cat actually likes going to the lake. He likes the ride, and he likes it when he gets there, and he likes helping us get rid of the mice and everything about it. I think what he doesn't like is being told what to do, that is, being told that he's going to the lake now, when he wasn't ready.

Once in a while, just once in a while, I say, "Let's go to the lake," and my wife says, "I can't go today or tomorrow. I've changed my hair appointment and my piano lesson, and I told Aunt Marian I'd take her to lunch tomorrow, and the day after that the people are coming to wash the windows and I'm going to start making my calls for the church." And on and on and on like that. "Why don't you go on down by yourself? You can take the dog and the cat for company and stay until Friday when we're due at the Olsens' at six."

Now then! This is what a Lakeside Retreat is really for! Contemplation! Total relaxation! Communion with Nature! No Piano Playing! Fishing, quietly and endlessly, just like on the calendar picture!

"Well, since I don't play golf or anything like that, I think I'll just do it! Keep your eye on the cat while I pack, and I'll be off."

Every once in a while it's fun to contemplate what you'd do if you were really completely alone in your lakeside retreat. You can sleep when you want to sleep, eat what you want whenever you want it, drink what you want whenever you want to, get drunk, in fact, if that's what you want to do, read a book or not read a book, play your favorite tapes as loud as you want, and just generally do whatever thing pops into your mind at the moment. It's sometimes an attractive thought.

I've thought that attractive thought lots of times, even though I know in my heart of hearts it's no good. Like Captain Tickle's rubber ball, when he cut it open, there was nothing there at all.

I learned long ago that total relaxation is something I really don't want. It sounds great, and I keep trying, but when I get right down to it, it's not so hot. There's nothing to do.

I have a really great speedboat, and I go boating. But speeding around the lake alone isn't all it's cracked up to be, and I get enough of it in about fifteen minutes. In fact, if I've been there alone long enough, I take the boat and go to the nearest floating bar and while away my time talking to the bartender there, which isn't exactly boating, as such, and is certainly something I could have done without going to all the trouble of driving three hours to the lake and getting the boat out and so forth.

In addition to the speedboat, I have a fishing boat. Now there's something to do! Go fishing!

This is another activity that is greatly overrated. Most people don't have the opportunity to spend a lot of time fishing. They have to go to a lot of trouble to lie to their wives and then buy a lot of beer and haul their boat to the lake and on and on like that, just to go fishing. These are the people to whom fishing seems attractive, those who never get the chance. I don't have to go to any trouble at all, but to me, fishing is a lot like doing nothing. Only you're doing nothing in an uncomfortable boat with a hard aluminum seat, and generally in the blazing sun, or else at some inconvenient hour like 6 a.m.

At the lake where I go, there are two basic ways to fish: actively and passively. Actively means casting for bass. You run the boat very slowly along near the bank and throw a plug or lure of some kind alongside the bank wherever you think there might be a bass. You can do this for hours, or until your arm runs out, and you catch a bass very, very infrequently.

The passive way is, you just sit in the boat over some spot where you think the fish are congregating and hold a pole with a hook and a worm on it and wait for a hungry and careless fish to come along. You tend to catch more fish by this method, but generally not so many that it keeps you very interested or excited for very long.

I no sooner find my spot and get my hook and worm in the water, then I start thinking about what I really should be doing instead of this. I should be trimming the bushes in front of the house or cutting limbs off the tree beside the walk or putting some new gravel on the driveway, or even going out in the speedboat to see the fellows at the floating bar. Pretty soon, if the fish aren't really just fighting over my worm and creating lots of excitement, my conscience gets the better of me and I realize I'd better be getting something done instead of just posing like this for a "Golden Years" calendar picture.

So that's the end of the fishing period.

Then I actually do accomplish a few chores, but not many. I clean out the work room so it'll be ready the next time I want to do some work, which is not right now.

I sit down and visit with the dog and the cat for a few minutes. There's not much new with them. The dog has already been boating and fishing with me, so I can't tell him any lies about how much fun I'd had.

I put a tape on the player. My wife and I don't always enjoy the same music, so when I'm alone at the lake I can play something I don't play at home. One thing I like that she hates is "Lucia," so I play that good and loud. I have a 90-minute tape of excerpts. Ninety minutes of "Lucia" highlights is a lot.

Now, at last, it's time for the cocktail hour and time to fix my dinner just the way I like it!

After dinner I read my book a while, then I figure I'd better call my wife to make sure she's getting along all right without me. She's not home, so I worry for a little while and then try her again.

I find she's getting along just fine; she's been to our daughter's house for dinner.

"How are you getting along?" she says. "Having fun?"

"Oh yeah. I've been out in the boat most of the day except

when I wasn't fishing, and I've really done a lot around here. Having a great time. But I think I'll come home tomorrow instead of waiting until Friday. I really do have a lot of things I should be doing at home."

And so that's what it's like to be retired and go to your lakeside retreat whenever you want to. Everyone ought to try it once in a while.

CHAPTER EIGHT

On Playing Golf

IF YOU'RE THINKING ABOUT RETIRING, one of the things you absolutely have to be willing to do is play golf. Otherwise you'd better not retire.

It's the only game I know of that most of the people who play it do so, not because they enjoy it, but because they have to. According to my friends who spend most of their time playing golf, it's not only no fun, but it's an unsettling, stressful, expensive and frustrating thing to do.

But they play it because it's an acceptable way to spend your time when you're retired, and because otherwise they wouldn't have a blessed thing to do at all.

Most people I know don't play golf in order to get better at it, like people do in most sports or games. In fact, they don't even want to get better because the handicapping system gives them a really big advantage if they play poorly. My brother-in-law who plays a lot of golf has steadily been getting worse for the past ten years, and he's delighted with this turn of events. It enables him to challenge and beat really good players. This doesn't make sense, but it's true.

You see a lot of former company presidents out playing golf day after day. generally these people have been successful businessmen; in fact, they must have been, since they can now afford to play this expensive, boring and time-consuming game.

But what they're really doing is gambling. That's what the real attraction is, but generally, so far as I've been able to see, the stakes are so very low it would hardly be worth a company president's time. I mean, they spend the entire day winning a dollar-forty. Then, because he won all that money, he has to stand the losing players to drinks in the clubhouse, and the drink tab runs to forty dollars. So he's out thirty-eight dollars and sixty cents because he won. This doesn't make sense either.

One thing about it that I think people like is the paraphernalia. First, there are the clubs. This is a whole long boring subject in itself. But you have to have really expensive clubs and a terribly heavy bag full of them, with a little plaque on it with your name and home course. Even the really no-good players, like my brother-in-law, have a set of clubs that make your eyes bug out. His are so heavy he can't even get them out of the trunk of his car by himself.

And then you have to worry about dressing properly. One thing about golf, you have to be really dressed for it with the latest slacks and golf shirts and so forth, and especially the shoes. The shoes have metal spikes so you can't wear them to do anything except play golf, and most of the players I know don't really need those spikes, but do you think they'd play in just regular comfortable walking shoes? Of course not.

Not that they walk anywhere anyway. the golfers I know just ride around in those little carts. I've tried that, and that part is fun for a few minutes.

The ongoing need for clothes and shoes and clubs and other accouterments for the game is partly what makes it so successful, especially for the wives and children of the golfers because that gives them something to give their golf-playing loved ones for Christmas. I don't even play golf, but I keep getting new golf shirts for my birthday.

Then one of the most expensive things connected to the game is belonging to a golf club, although that is really just the beginning of the expense. It's an anomaly, but I myself belong to an expensive golf club, even though I never play the game. I belong because I keep thinking I'm going to start playing and buy one of those huge golf bags with my name on it and so forth. I have a friend who also belongs to that same club and who also doesn't play golf. Occasionally we get dressed up in our Christmas golf clothes and go out and eat lunch with the golfers and pretend we're like the big boys. We sit around with them and drink gin and play gin rummy and say dirty words just like they do, but it isn't all that much fun. I'm glad to come home and get out of those fancy duds.

But if you don't play golf, you have to do something else, and one of the things I sometimes do when I can't avoid it is cut the grass. Now there's a challenge! Around where I live, the grass needs cutting at least once a week during the early summer growing season. Starting around the 4th of July, it dries up and looks terrible, so you don't need to cut it any more. But the early summer is a different story, and you have to either be johnny-on-the-spot or else have some yard crew that is.

When I was younger and more agile, strong and sleek, I always hired somebody to cut my grass even though I could have done it myself. Now that I'm retired, however, my wife thinks it's wasteful to hire somebody to cut it when I'm perfectly healthy and just sitting around the house, not playing golf. And I have to admit she's got something there. For several seasons a few years ago, the lawn service sent a lady out to cut my grass, and I felt absolutely terrible about sitting around watching her do it.

Anyway, cutting the grass is now one of my chores, and I will admit to doing a lot better job of it than the lawn service people do who don't care any more about my lawn than they do about any of their other customers' lawns.

But in my neighborhood most of the other houses have been bought by young folks, and my wife and I are the oldest people on the block. And, of course, all these young fellows — doctors on the way up and so forth — have lawn services that cut their grass. So there I am out cutting my grass, and every other house on the block has a lawn service truck parked out in front, and I'm the only homeowner doing his own lawn.

Here I am, formerly a pretty big deal around town and in my business life, now I'm just going back and forth, back and forth, behind my lawnmower, while all my young neighbors are shelling out all this money to have somebody else do it. Is this what I saved and scraped for? Is this honorable retirement?

That's what's so really great about golf. The oldsters can go out there and swing and hack and sweat and swear, and everybody thinks they're having fun. That's what they've been working toward all their lives. Well, I can tell you, a lot of them would just as soon be home cutting their grass if it were an acceptable thing to do, which it's not.

In the wintertime I don't like to hang around this sleety, grimy, freezing city, so my wife and I have been looking around at various different places to go where it's warm, and where we can while away the chilly months of our golden years.

We've tried several different spots, and do you know, there is absolutely no place you can go unless you play golf all the time? Golf courses have taken over most every pleasant warm spot in this country.

We've spent several wintry months living in golf course communities in warm places like southern California and Arizona. But since we don't play golf, there's absolutely nothing to do at a place like that except eat and drink. We go to their cocktail parties in the evening, and all the men discuss is the bunker on the seventh hole and the green on the ninth hole, and how they are never again going to pick up a golf club, and how so-and-so lost a dollar forty-nine to so-and-so and how crowded the golf course is and what a pain it is to have a tee-time at 8 a.m. and so forth. We come home from a party like that, and my wife says, "Did you have a good time?" and I just say, "Muggins to you, too."

In those sunny golf course communities, golf gets to be a really dangerous game. For one thing, there are so very many old people, I mean really old people (not people like me), and they're all out there sweating in the sun in their Nile blue golf shirts and matching slacks, when they really should be home in bed. I think at the more expensive places they have an ambulance standing by near the ninth green to welcome some elderly former company president who just lost a dollar forty-seven on the front nine and had a heart attack as a result.

The other dangerous thing about it is that in a sunny land like that it's almost impossible to stay out of the sun and play golf at the same time. Every course should have its own dermatologist, and if I were a young dermatologist, that's where I'd head for. He'd be in a dermatologist's hog heaven just treating the arms and hands of the golfers, particularly the lady golfers who finally get to looking like they'd spent their lives herding sheep in the Australian outback.

Of course, I just say that from a retired company president's point of view, there are a lot of good features to being a regular golf player. The main one is that it's a lot like going to the office used to be. You can get up in the morning, put on your fancy clothes and say, "Good-bye, dear, I'm going to be gone all day."

In today's world, however, this doesn't work too well, even though it used to be perfect. Today, when you get up and say that, your wife is very apt to say, "My foursome is playing today, too. Let's just eat at the club tonight."

CHAPTER NINE

My Trip to Washington

My wife and daughter in Washington

BEING RETIRED, OR EVEN SEMI-RETIRED, means you're hanging around the house a lot more than you used to be, with not much to do. So I was excited at the prospect of a real outing when my wife told me we were going to Washington.

Not Washington, D.C., of course, not **that** much of an outing, but Washington, Missouri.

I looked it up on the map. "It's near St. Louis," I said. "What fun! The Arch! Anthony's for dinner! The Chase-Park Plaza!"

"Yes," my wife said, "but we're not going to St. Louis. Just to Washington. You'll like it because it's where they used to make corncob pipes before tobacco got such a bad name."

"I don't know anybody in Washington," I said.

"You'll be meeting some of them," she said.

The way it came up was like this: we have a daughter who lives in Denver. This daughter has been asked to be in the wedding of a friend whose parents live in Washington, Missouri. And since our daughter is going to be a bridesmaid, we got invited to the wedding even though we don't know the bride or her parents or anybody else in Washington. And furthermore, since we haven't seen our daughter for a little while, my wife thought it might be a nice outing for us to drive to Washington, go to the wedding and see our daughter all in one crack.

I have more or less given up going to weddings of my children's friends. With the divorce rate what it is, I feel I have been wearing out my tuxedo unnecessarily, going to all these weddings that are likely to end in divorce before my suit even comes back from the cleaners.

But this particular wedding in Washington had an additional complicating factor that made it desirable, even necessary, for us to make the trip.

Our daughter, as a bridesmaid, had to wear a special bridesmaid outfit. A couple of months before the wedding my wife had received a package in the mail from Washington that contained some material and a dress pattern. With it came instructions from the bride's mother to hand this material to her dressmaker and have our daughter's dress made, so she'd match the other girls.

Well, do you think my wife would hand that material to a dressmaker? Of course not. With a little cry of exultation, she went upstairs and shut herself in the sewing room for a couple of weeks and came out with a bridesmaid dress. I knew nothing about Washington, Missouri, at the time, but I envisioned the other bridesmaids' mothers there, sitting in that quiet, tree-shaded central Missouri community, happily sewing away, probably on a treadle sewing machine.

Was I ever wrong about that! Every bridesmaid's mother in Washington had lost no time in getting that material into the hands of the fanciest dressmakers in St. Louis., Our daughter's dress turned out to be the only one that was home-made, and it was something of a wonder when that fact became known in quiet, rural, tree-shaded Washington.

Anyway, because our daughter lives in Denver and she hadn't been around when my wife was making her dress, my wife just had to guess at things like her measurements. And that's why we had to go to Washington, so she could try it on before the wedding and we'd know for sure it would fit. The opportunity for exciting outings like this ought to make everyone wish he was retired like I am.

So what we did was, first we had to take the sewing machine apart. It's not portable or anything easy like that, but it is possible to unscrew it from its permanent base and pack it in the car, along with all the necessary parts and bobbins and threads and everything else, including the ironing board.

Then we get to drive to Washington. It's a pretty drive, along the river, and on the way you go through a small town called Hermann, Missouri, which is supposed to be an interesting, quaint little place where the descendants of the original German settlers make wine.

This is where I locked the keys in the car. In the hottest part of the afternoon, in the blazing sun on the main street of Hermann, we got out to stretch our legs and try a sip of local wine. The engine of the car was running, and so was the air conditioner, and my wife and I were both walking into the wine shop when I realized I'd locked the keys in the car. In that instant I also remembered that when I'd bought the car the salesman had explained to me that it was "virtually theft-proof," and that nobody could get in unless they broke a window. One of the great selling points.

It may be "virtually theftproof if the car's not running, but I am here to tell you that it's possible, just barely, to snake a very thin piece of metal through the window wing, and after about an hour of working and sweating in the boiling sun, if you're really lucky you can get the thin piece of metal in touch with the button that opens the electric window. Then, if you're careful not to have a heart attack or a heat stroke, and if by extreme good chance you have left the engine running, you can finally touch the window button with the strip of metal and lower the window enough to get your arm into the car and unlock the damned door. We skipped the wine shop then, and gladly got into the pre-cooled car and drove on to Washington.

We found the motel easily; it's the only motel in Washington. And then we unloaded the ironing board and the sewing machine and all the other things needed to fit the dress, and then we waited for the daughter to show up. I felt like one of those itinerant Hong Kong tailors that set up shop in a hotel room and sell suits.

Finally she showed up, tried on the dress and, not surprisingly, knowing my wife, it fit pretty well. Just about an hour's worth of readjustments were needed. After that we had time for the cocktail hour before going to the seven o'clock wedding.

At six o'clock it rained, really hard. The heavens opened up and dumped the entire thing on Washington, Missouri. I knew that the reception was to be in the bride's parents' back yard, and I felt sorry for them. But I underestimated Washington.

The wedding was in a beautiful 19th century church overlooking the river in downtown Washington. There was a harpist imported for the occasion from the St. Louis Philharmonic. And all the bridesmaids looked really great in their matching outfits.

And then the drive through the dripping evening to the bride's parents' house for the reception. And what a beautiful spot! Five acres of lawn adjoining the golf course and overlooking the river. Tables and chairs for four-hundred guests. A really great band under a giant tent. And an army of caterers and helpers and waiters and cooks, and people to park your car and everything dry as a chip, even though the rain had drenched everything just an hour or so earlier.

There were bars everywhere, and people passing champagne, and a truck loaded with beer on tap, and then later a really marvelous dinner cooked right there on the spot, and all in all I couldn't think of anything that was missing. We didn't get to visit much with our daughter who was dancing with some other young person most of the evening, but never mind, just as my wife had said, we got to meet a lot of people from Washington, and we fell in love with them all. My wife became something of a celebrity among the Washington ladies for having made the bridesmaid outfit all by herself.

When we finally tucked it in that night, I told my wife it had indeed been a wonderful outing. So, if you ever get invited to a wedding in Washington, jump at the chance.

CHAPTER TEN

The Mouse That Roared

Cute mouse and cute raccoon in our kitchen

AS YOU SLOWLY DODDER through the Golden Years of your retirement, every once in a while your weekends are illuminated by a visit from your children. In the case of children who live out of town, these visits are greatly facilitated if you send them the money for the plane tickets.

Every once in a while my wife says, "We don't have anything much doing for the next few weeks; let's see if the girls don't want to come over for the weekend." That's the signal for me to send them the money for the plane tickets. Then she adds, "Maybe they'd like to take a few things back with them."

When our children left home, they did just that, and no more. That is, they just left home, walked out, and left most of their worldly goods in the bedrooms in our house, thinking perhaps their marriages wouldn't last or, more likely, that we would clean it all out and send it to them, which we have not done. So it's exciting to have them come to town and sit around in their old rooms laughing at their old photo albums and high school annuals before putting them back into their desks again and going off to see their friends.

One of the things they do when I pay for their plane tickets to come visit me is they spend most of their time visiting their friends. I know they're in town because their old photo albums are piled all over their bedrooms, and some of the clothes they left in their closets four years ago are strewn all over their beds. But the girls themselves, along with their husbands, are out visiting friends. Sometimes they leave a grandchild behind for my wife to watch while they're gone, as a token of their trust in us.

But the main activity, the principal purpose of their visit, is to go with us to our old lakeside retreat. For many years we've had a cabin on a lake near here, and when the children were young, my wife and I would pop them into the car on Friday evenings and take them to the lake where we spent the weekends amongst the poison ivy and the illegal-size fish and the tepid water of an artificial Midwestern lake. Nowadays when they fly in to visit us, one of the things they, and we, like to do is go to the lake and re-create their childhood victories over nature and demonstrate their continued skill at water skiing. The husbands, not having been brought up with this particular lake, would rather be doing something else, but they're good-natured about the whole thing, and have even become good water skiers themselves.

So we pack up the food and the beer and other essentials

and drive to the lake, arriving after dark on Friday night.

The house has been closed and locked up for several weeks, and the moment we walk in, we know we're in trouble.

Any closed house in the woods beside a lake in a Midwestern summer attracts mice. That's acceptable, or at least understandable and handleable. The country mice, unaccustomed to life-threatening situations, are easy to catch in a trap on your first night there.

But it is not acceptable if one of the mice has died, especially in the kitchen. And that was very obviously what had happened during our absence. You could tell it the moment you stepped into the house.

I said, "Open all the windows quickly and let this smell out."

One of the girls said, "I think Larry and I will sleep in the guest house."

Larry, one of the sons-in-law, said, "Surely there's a nice motel nearby."

But we opened all the windows and began thinking of something else, and pretty soon we were able to walk around in the kitchen without noticing the smell too strongly. By sitting outside on the deck we even managed to forget it for a few minutes. A two-year-old grandchild, awake far too late in the evening in my opinion, was sternly advised by his mother not to totter too near that part of the kitchen most richly affected by the odor, and where he might run into, and innocently try to eat, a dead mouse.

My wife and I sleep in another part of the house, far away from the kitchen. And the girls elected to take their husbands and child and sleep in the guest house. Even though their old rooms in the house exert a strong emotional pull, that pull couldn't overcome the smell of the mouse which seemed to sneak through the walls into those sentimental bedrooms.

The next morning broke bright and sunny and breezy, and the lure of the outdoor activities was stronger than the odor.

We left all the doors and windows open and went outdoors to play, temporarily forgetting the problem in the kitchen. That night we cooked the dinner outside over charcoal and ate it on the deck, again managing to avoid the mouse problem which was hanging over us.

The following morning, another problem surfaced. I was the first one up, and I held my nose and went into the kitchen to make coffee. There, facing me on the kitchen counter, were four clean peach pits and one half-eaten pear. I had also been the last person awake the night before, and those peaches and that pear had been left neatly placed in a small basket on the counter, in preparation for breakfast. And now, nothing remained of them except the pits, and lots of filthy little footprints all over the counter. From past experience, I realized that we had been invaded by raccoons during the night, and that something had to be done. The smell of the dead mouse was stronger than ever, and now, somehow, raccoons had found their way into the house. The weekend wasn't turning out the way I had hoped.

This particular morning was damp and dark, not one to lure us out onto the lake. So I said, "We have to do something about that mouse and something about that raccoon."

My wife said, "It certainly does smell in here." And the girls said, "We'll all do it together."

So, using our noses, we decided which cupboards had to be attacked first. All the canned goods came out, all the spices, all the pots and pans and dishes and miscellaneous kitchen equipment, everything. Every cupboard was carefully inspected and washed, new shelf paper put in, and no mouse cadaver was discovered. This was a lot of work, with nothing to show for it except clean cupboards.

My wife, who has a very sharp nose, said, "I think it must be in the stove." So the electric stove was emptied out, the cooking utensils underneath all removed, the drawers opened, new shelf paper installed. Still no mouse's remains. So the stove has to be pulled out from its niche against the wall. This takes everybody pulling all at once. And then the back of the stove has to be removed. This is not easy, probably fifty different metal screws are involved, many different metal plates, and lots of sniffing and smelling and agreeing that "we're getting somewhere." But after the stove had been thoroughly dismantled to the point where I was sure we could never get it back together again, and left standing alone in the middle of the room, my wife said, "That's funny. The stove doesn't smell any more. There's no dead mouse in the stove. It has to be somewhere else."

Adjacent to the stove are drawers which we have already cleaned out, but which still smell. "It must be underneath those drawers," one of the sons-in-law asserts. So the drawers have to come out again and, as owner of the house, I get to saw a hole in the floor beneath a drawer.

Everybody takes turns smelling at the hole in the floor. "Sweet as a baby's breath" is the general consensus. So, where in the world do we go from there?"

From my place on the floor behind the stove, the odor was especially strong, and in using my nose carefully, I followed it to the electrical outlet on the wall where the stove is normally hooked up. And the smell around this outlet seemed to be especially terrible.

Again, everybody took turns smelling at the wall near the floor behind the stove. This is not easy to do. It requires a lot of cooperation and a good deal of companionship, since you have to climb over each other to get in or out. And again, as the owner of the house, I got the privilege of sawing a hole in the wall beside the electrical outlet. The moment I got that hole started, I knew I'd struck it rich; the smell was awful, just what I'd hoped for.

Anyway, we finally found the mouse after sawing a giant hole in the wall. Only it wasn't a tiny mouse at all, but a largish pack-rat, not a real rat, but his country cousin, a playful pack rat, and a fairly recently dead one. That smell would have lingered for months. And here was the kitchen, a complete shambles, with pieces of the stove stashed everywhere, a hole in the floor, a largish hole in the wall, pots and pans piled high, the girls busily washing years of grease off the stove, and everybody happy at our victory over troublesome nature.

It took another hour to get the various holes patched up again and the stove put back together and reinstalled, and the kitchen settled back down to a sweet-smelling place where you could cook and eat. Then it took another hour of everybody working together to locate the hole where the raccoon came in. Far up against the house under a small deck on the back, one of the girls found a perfect raccoon-size hold. Then with much squirming and crawling and cooperating, we managed to nail it closed. So, a great victory, too, over the raccoon.

After that, there was still some playtime left, so the girls and husbands had a triathlon. They all jogged down the road to the end of the point, maybe two miles, where I met them in the boat and collected their shoes. Then they swam back to the dock, a distance of maybe a half-mile, then they took turns on the skis. By this time, the day was over, and I'm sure they were exhausted. I know I was.

That evening after dinner, everybody sat around and congratulated each other on what a wonderful day it had been. How it had been just so much fun all day long, how overcoming obstacles is what life is all about, how they were so glad they'd made the trip and how much fun it is to come and see the grandparents. And especially how it's a really great feeling to have finally found that mouse.

And that evening as we were sitting around the table, slightly beery, the girls started singing old songs from their childhood. They harmonized beautifully with their mother; the three voices still sound wonderful together.

One of them started singing "Juanita." I don't know if you're familiar with "Juanita" or not, but it's a sentimental old chestnut from way back before my time. Here's how the chorus goes:

"Nita, Juanita, ask they soul if we should part;
Nita, Juanita, lean thou on my heart."

For some reason, we had taught it to the girls when they were little, and they seemed to like to harmonize to it. I said, "I haven't thought of that oldie for twenty years. I'm amazed you remember it."

One of them said that it's one of her favorites. And the other one said it's one of the songs she sings to her little boy as a lullaby, and it's one of his favorites, and he's learning the tune.

So, sometime in the 21st century, among the sooty towers of faraway Denver, there will be a tall blond young man, a grandson of mine, if you can believe it, going about his business, while under his breath singing, "Nita, Juanita, lean thou on my heart." It may not seem like a very big deal to you, but to me it's a real accomplishment.

It even tops finding a dead mouse in the wall.

CHAPTER ELEVEN

Everybody Ought to Go to Washington

Yours truly at the monument

THE OTHER DAY I WAS HANGING AROUND the house, quietly enjoying my Golden Years when my wife said, "Everybody ought to go to Washington." Offhand, I couldn't think of a smart comeback. The next time I saw her, which was several hours later, after her piano lesson and her aerobics workout, she said it again.

Then I said, "Only kooks and freaks go to Washington. We're better off staying here. We'd probably get mugged."

Then she reminded me that we have a daughter who lives

in Washington. We haven't seen this daughter for some time, and my wife thought it would be nice to combine a tourist trip to Washington with a visit to our daughter who is working for a lady lawmaker there. My wife said, "Here are some great, inexpensive, conveniently-timed airplane tickets to Washington," and she showed me the tickets she'd bought. "We don't have much else to do, so let's go to Washington."

I had been to Washington before, of course, on business. Not business with the White House or anything like that, but just ordinary private-sector business, where you get off the airplane, go to a meeting at some nearby hotel and get back on the airplane a couple of days later. In other words, I'd been there, but I hadn't seen it.

And now I'm here to tell you, everybody ought to go to Washington. Next to Disneyland and Disney World, it's the greatest place in this country to be a tourist, and it's considerably cheaper, too.

We didn't get mugged at all. In fact, I felt pretty safe, even though where we were staying wasn't the Ritz Carlton, and we walked all over the place late at night and took the subway everywhere. My Washington daughter does all those things all the time and probably much worse, and she seems to have survived.

And the downtown part of Washington where tourists go is really pretty compact and convenient and handy to everything, and it's not hard at all to get around, and everybody seems helpful, and it's almost impossible to get lost. And there are taxis everywhere that are reasonably inexpensive, and the fares are standardized. If you get tired of walking, you can just get a cab and go back to your hotel and take off your shoes, which I did from time to time.

The Disneyland part is this really great Mall right in front of the capitol. You take one of these little tour buses that run all the time, and you go from one end of the mall to the other. You get out at the attractions you want to see, including the

Capitol, the White House, the Washington Monument, the Lincoln Memorial, the Viet Nam Memorial, the Smithsonian, the National Gallery, everything. And it's all free, and there's always a tour just starting, and they have these bright, attractive young guides who seem to know all about everything. And they have other people out there sweeping up your cigarette butts, just like in Disneyland. It's all very well organized and efficient and educational and clean. I didn't see a single mugger.

And, of course, the attractions are first-rate. I mean, the tour of the Capitol is impressive, interesting and fun; likewise, of course, the White House and the Justice Department and the Library of Congress and so on. But, in addition, there are all these non-government things that the government runs such as the National Gallery, the Natural History Museum, the Hirschorn Gallery, the Aviation and Space Museum and more, which are all parts of the Smithsonian. (Your tax dollars at work.)

And they're merely the greatest attractions of their kind in the whole world. You could spend a whole day or a whole week in the National Gallery if you're so inclined, or in the Natural History Museum or the Space Museum or most of the others along that row. And they're all free. It's terrific.

Those are the standard tourist kind of things in Washington, and they're great. But part of the fun of Washington is just being in Washington. For instance, we went to an Ethiopian restaurant which I'm never going to do again, but which I'm glad now that I've done once. And you don't find Ethiopian restaurants just everywhere. There's not a single one in my home town, for instance, although there are lots in Washington. At an Ethiopian restaurant you eat with your fingers which is a giant step backwards in my opinion, eating stone age food in stone age fashion just like they did in the desert way before the dark ages, before they invented forks. But my daughter said it was one of the big trendy things to do in Washington right now, and sure enough, all the trendy people were there eating with their fingers, and it really wasn't all that bad. The sushi bars are still busy, too. Apparently there are enough trendy people to keep all the trendy ethnic places going.

We had a great Italian meal, too. My wife and I just recently returned from Italy, so that's something we know about, and our Italian meal in Washington could easily have been served to us in Siena or Florence, only it was a lot cheaper in Washington.

We did things like taking the elevator to the top of the Washington Monument. I know it sounds corny, but it was fun. And we took a nice hike to the Tomb of the Unknown Soldier at Arlington Cemetery, and we walked along the length of the Viet Nam Memorial. We stood along with all the other tourists in the Lincoln Memorial reading the Gettysburg Address which is carved in stone there, and which is really terrific, especially considering, as the old joke goes, that Lincoln wrote it while traveling from Washington to Gettysburg on the back of an envelope.

Seriously, I was impressed by all these things. We were at the Lincoln Memorial on an absolutely lovely fall day, and there were lots of other people there when we were. They were a really diverse group, racially, sociologically, economically, and every other way you can think of. And we all stood quietly inside that monument, and for the briefest fraction of a second we were all one.

Most everybody in Washington speaks English, although not all, by a long shot. There are tourists there not only from every state in the U.S., but from probably every country in the world. The people at the top of the Washington Monument with us were speaking Japanese and German and French and something else I couldn't figure out. As usual, the French people pushed ahead and got on the elevator first.

Among the people who don't speak English are the cab drivers, which sometimes creates a little problem. Apparently the new American citizens who have most recently come from some place else now start out in this country by driving a cab in Washington instead of working in the steel mills in Gary, Indiana, the way they used to. We didn't encounter one native American cab driver while we were there, but we always managed to communicate okay, and he always got us to the right place, which is more than I could have done. The people who served us in the Ethiopian restaurant were Ethiopians, I think, but the waiter in the Italian place was from Iran. I asked him.

There's a feeling of excitement in the air in Washington, and you can't get away from it. Even the place where we stayed was sharing in the excitement. Through some friends of my wife we stayed at a private club that offers a few hotel rooms. It's called the Sulgrave Club which sounds fancier than it is, and the gimmick is that it's a private club for ladies only. Well, a few doors down the street is another private club called the Cosmos Club which is for men only. And lately, in the Washington papers there's been this big brouhaha about whether the Cosmos Club has to start admitting women. So, of course, the Sulgrave Club gets in the papers, too, because somebody is saying that the Sulgrave has to start admitting men, and it's a big editorial-page tiff between the male columnists and the women columnists, and here we are, right in the middle of all the excitement!

Sitting back at home reading the papers, I get pretty disillusioned about some of the sleazy things that go on in Washington, and I suppose it's all true. But because of my attractive daughter who was showing us around, we got invited to a Washington party, and I met some of the people who are helping to run the government.

This was a party given by some young people from our home town for other young people from our home town who are currently working in Washington, and there are quite a few of them. Most of the people at the party were working for the government somehow — some were aides or lower-level assistants to congressmen, others were working in the Justice

Department, or on various sub-committee staffs, and some were working for lobbyists and on and on. Talking to all these young people was heartening for me. They were bright, articulate, interested, knowledgeable, sincere, devoted and hard-working. Yet they were understanding, willing to listen, willing to compromise, able to see both sides of things and, I thought, thoroughly entertaining and valuable people to have working in your government. Part of them, I felt, were pretty far to the right and others were pretty far to the left, but the great bulk of them seemed to be pretty close to the middle which is where I stand, along with most of the rest of the American people. At this party, with all these bright young people, of course, my wife and I were by far the oldest guests. And I was the only person who smoked; that tells you something.

When I got back home after my trip, I said to my wife, "Everybody ought to go to Washington."

CHAPTER TWELVE

Winter Wonderland

The worst blizzard I have ever seen

THE OTHER DAY MY WIFE SAID TO ME, "Since you're retired now and don't have much to do, let's go down and relax
for a few days at our lakeside retreat."

I was a little surprised at this because it was the dead of
winter, and there's not much to do at our lakeside retreat in
the dead of winter except eat and drink and take an occasional walk in the woods. But she said, "A few days of relaxation will lower your blood pressure and maybe increase your
life expectancy and help us get rid of our colds by taking long
naps," and so on.

I'm always eager to go to our lakeside retreat no matter
what the weather, so we packed up the car and the dog and
the cat and the vacuum sweeper which we'd had at home

getting repaired, and a few other things, and drove to the lake on an unusually balmy Sunday afternoon in December.

We knew that our daughter and her husband and their little boy were already there at the lakeside retreat, having spent the weekend there. The plan was that my wife and I would go down and eat dinner with them on Sunday night; then they'd strap their little boy into his government-mandated safety seat in their car and drive on home. Unlike me, my son-in-law is not retired, so he has to go to work on Monday mornings.

So that was the way it worked out. My wife and I arrived, we played choo-choo with the grandson for a little while, then we ate dinner and they packed up and drove on home. Then, after the dishes were done, and the effects of playing choo-choo had worn off, I got the chance to sit around quietly and start lowering my blood pressure. Except that there was this country mouse that kept running around the rooms startling us every once in a while. But with what I was sure was a healthy low blood pressure reading, we went to bed in a frigid bedroom and turned on the electric blanket and slept peacefully for a good straight eight.

When we woke up, I looked out at the worst blizzard I have ever seen. The snow had crept in during the night, and the woods were already pure white, and the lake down in front of the house was pure black, and the lane which leads for a quarter of a mile from our house to the nearest paved road was already invisible.

"If we're going to get out of here before Christmas, we have to leave right now," I said.

"Don't be silly," she said. "This is what we came for. It's ideal for relaxing. Build a big fire and we'll start relaxing right away."

"Do we have enough food?" I said.

"Enough," she said enigmatically, without looking up from her knitting.

So I built a big fire, and the dog and I mushed out through

the snow and brought in a lot of big logs, and we all sat around and relaxed. The snow kept on coming down in great big wet flakes and piling up all around us.

As the day wore on, I found it harder and harder to relax. I was reading a book, but I kept losing my place from gazing out at the snow falling and wondering what was going to happen to us.

We were counting on going to the store to get some food that morning. We didn't bring much of anything from home, and the grocery store is fairly convenient under normal circumstances. In spite of what my wife had said, I knew we didn't have much to eat. Not knowing where my next meal is coming from tends to worry me. Not being able to get to the grocery store is a very worrisome proposition, since I'm pretty accustomed to regular meals. I've never seen it snow so continuously. The dog and I continued to go out and bring in more wood, although my feet were soaking wet because when we left home it was so balmy I didn't bring anything but canvas jogging shoes.

Pretty soon, staring out the window, I said, "I have a date for lunch in town tomorrow with my accountant."

My wife said, "I'd cancel it if I were you. Better put another log on the fire." So I called long distance and canceled my lunch date for the next day, which didn't make me feel any better.

You have to understand that our lakeside retreat is pretty remote, even in the summer. But in the winter, it's really nowheresville, with no other houses around for a couple of miles in all directions. We've always liked it this way, that is, up until now. And you have to understand, too, that our house is very old and rickety, and we're at the far end of the electric power line, and the power company is one of those country rural electrification outfits that supplies power when they feel like it, and that without power the furnace won't run, and the water supply is from a well that's served by an electric pump.

If the electricity goes off, we not only don't have any heat, but we don't have any water, and there's nobody to call in case we run into any kind of trouble. Nobody could get to us even if we could call somebody and, of course, we can't possibly get out of here because our car is buried so deep we can't even see it. Even if we could find the car, we couldn't possibly drive up to the highway through the deep snow. And here I am, relaxing and lowering my blood pressure. Instead, I'm certain it has climbed sharply.

I put on my soaking wet tennis shoes and my light nylon jacket and tramped my way down to the lake to see how the dock was doing. It was sinking. Normally it floats high on big blocks of styrofoam, but the snow on the roof had gotten so heavy that the floor of the dock was almost under water.

When I came back, I said to my wife, "Think what that heavy snow is doing to the roof of this old house. It could give way any minute." She kept right on knitting.

Then I said, "I wonder how much longer we'll have electricity." She didn't say anything.

Then I said, "If the power goes out, we won't have any water either." She didn't say anything.

Pretty soon I said, "With every inch of new snow, my blood pressure goes up ten points."

She said, "In the meadow we can build a snow man."

"And pretend that he is Parson Brown," I said, "and that he's in the tow-truck business on the side."

On dark days late in December, you can't tell when night comes. But sometime late in the evening it stopped snowing. The dog and I mushed up to where I thought the car was, and I shoveled some of the snow off of it. But it didn't look too promising as a means of transportation.

"I found a can of corned beef for our dinner," my wife said when I came back again. "It's only a couple of years old, so it's probably still good."

"Wonderful," I said.

We ate the corned beef and went to bed under the electric blanket. I fully expected it to go off, along with the rest of the power, in the middle of the night, but it didn't.

In the morning everything was beautiful. Beautiful to look at, I mean. Many of the cedar trees were bent double under the weight of the beautiful snow. My tennis shoes had partly dried out in the night. We ate some more corned beef, and the dog and I walked up the lane to look at the paved road to see if it had been plowed. It hadn't. In order to walk up our lane I had to shake the overhanging trees free of snow. A real Winter Wonderland.

I came back and cleaned off the car and finally started the engine. I drove up the lane about twenty feet before I was stuck fast. It was my wife's car, so she came out and tried it, too, but she didn't do any better. By that time, both of us were cold and wet, so we went back and sat in front of the fire, not relaxing, just getting warm.

Since my shoes were already wet, I decided to let my fingers do the walking, and I started calling numbers in the slim local Yellow Pages under "Wreckers." Eventually I got a nice warm-sounding voice in a garage thirty miles away who said somewhat guardedly that he had a wrecker and he would come in a couple of hours and "look the situation over." I set my shoes in front of the fire and started making mental notes of all the things I should be doing right now in the city.

After a couple of hours and a few upticks in my blood pressure, I went outside hoping to meet the wrecker man as he drove down the lane. When I got to where the car was stuck, I met the wrecker man walking down the lane toward me through the deep snow. I was very glad to see him. But he had left his wrecker parked up on the paved road.

He looked the car over very carefully, and then he said in that warm voice, "Mister, if I were to drive my wrecker down to where your car is, I wouldn't even be able to drive the wrecker out, much less tow your car. The snow is just too deep, and the lane is too steep." So much for the warm voice.

"What's going to happen to me?" I asked, casually clutching at his sleeve. "Surely you're not just going to go away and leave us here!"

He thought for a few minutes and then said, "I almost brought some chains that might fit your car, but I didn't. With chains, you might be able to drive out by yourself."

When he said that, a small light bulb turned on in my head. "Come to think of it, I might have some chains myself, right in the back of that car! Seems to me my son-in-law bought some chains for this car last winter. I've never used them, but they might still be here." Then with nervous frozen fingers I searched through the car and found a box of new tire chains, almost unused.

"What do you know! Look at this," I said. "I had chains in here all along."

The warm-voiced wrecker man said, "Great. I'll put them on for you." And he did, but not without a lot of trouble and lying down in the snow under the car and so forth. Then he said, "Get your wife, and I'll make sure you can drive out of here."

So I hurried into the house, and my wife and I rushed around and packed up everything and did what we had to do to close the place. We located the cat where he was hiding under a bed, and my wife carried him out to the car along with the litter box and so forth, and we persuaded the dog to hop into the car. I started the car and put it into forward gear and slammed on the gas, and we drove up the lane about thirty miles an hour, never slowing down until we reached the paved road, which incidentally had been plowed in the meantime. Then the wrecker man caught up with us and took off the chains, and I paid him and thanked him profusely, and we drove on home.

On the way home we made a list of the things we'd left down there in our hurry to get out, which included my wettest shoes.

So, if you ever retire and go to your lakeside retreat in the dead of winter in order to rest and relax and lower your blood pressure, be sure you have some canned corned beef on hand. It makes into good hash if you also have a potato and an onion, and if the electricity hasn't gone off.

CHAPTER THIRTEEN

A Walk in the Park

Newlyweds ascending

NOW THAT I'M REALLY RETIRED and don't get the exercise of going to the office any more, I have successfully matured from a size "medium" to a size "portly." Partly as a result of this, and partly because I don't have anything else very time-consuming or important to do, such as playing golf, I have learned to enjoy my daily walk. I take a walk every day.

Where I walk is in the park near my house, and I know that doesn't sound very exciting, but you'd be surprised.

I've always lived near this park, or ever since I can remember. When I was young and struggling, we lived on the east side of the park where the houses are small and inexpensive. The moment I started to get on my feet financially and was successfully making the payments on the small house where we lived, my wife decided to move to the west side of the park where the houses are bigger and more expensive. So we bought one and started making bigger payments, and we've lived there ever since, and both the house and I have outlived the mortgage, and the kids are grown and gone, but the park is still there.

Long before it was the thing to do, I was running. I was the only person doing it, and people thought I was nuts. But not very many people saw me doing it, because I ran around the park at 6:30 a.m. (In those days that big mortgage got me going very early every morning.) And I mean every morning — summer, winter, spring and fall. If the path around the park was too icy in the dead of winter, I was afraid I might fall in the dark and nobody would find me, so there were a few days, very few, that I missed. But by and large I ran every day for about eighteen years, and I do think that daily activity delayed my becoming a size "portly" for a few years at least.

The house where I live is just a few blocks from the park. The total distance from my front door to the park and around the park and back to my front door is almost exactly a mile and a half. This is no big deal by today's standards when young couples feel they've had a misspent day unless they've run their daily five miles, but in those days a mile-and-half run was regarded as a pretty good way to start the morning.

In those earlier days I ran with my brother every morning. That was before he got deaf and had knee surgery and became a "portly" and all that. Thirty years ago he took his family to Switzerland and they all climbed the Matterhorn together, and to get himself ready for the trip, he ran around the park with me every morning. It must have helped him because he made it to the top right alongside his teenage kids, but when he came back he felt he didn't need to run any more.

Nowadays, I walk with my dog. This is a very elderly female German Shepherd, and this dog has walked around the park every day of her life, or almost. She is the third dog I've walked with; the other two are both long dead. I've outlived and outwalked them, and this present one is showing signs of wear and walks a little slower every year. Growing old has made me a "portly," but growing old has made her a "slim Jim," and I worry about her. But right now she still wants to go, and I'm glad to have her.

The park where I walk which is just a few blocks from my house used to be a golf course many years ago. It belongs to the city now, but it still looks like a golf course, right in the middle of a busy metropolitan area, and for me it's the perfect place to walk.

I always follow the same route, every day. My wife thinks that's crazy, that we ought to vary our walk, but the dog and I are used to it.

We start at the southwest corner which is nearest our house, and we walk around the park counter-clockwise. First we walk by the war memorial. This is the Civil War. There was a minor skirmish here which didn't even make the history books, but one of our civic-minded banks put up a memorial anyway. Past the war memorial we continue along the south edge of the park to the southeast corner which is the highest ground in the park, where it's always windy and chilly. To add a little romance, I call it "Windy Point." From here you can see the big high-rise apartments downtown. Then the path turns north, and we walk down the hill toward the lake.

It's a good-sized lake for a city park, and it must have been a really tough water hazard in the days when the park was a golf course. It has a little island in it, and ducks and swans, and a quaint Japanese bridge and weeping willows and all that. In the old days when I was running at 6:30 in the mornings, I was almost always the first person in the park. During a few weeks in the spring, early in the morning I'd frequently run across a duck egg, evidently layed during the night on a flat rock and, of course, I'd take the egg home for my breakfast. Some mornings I'd find two. My wife didn't like the idea, but those duck eggs were lots fresher than the store-bought hens' eggs she was having. Nowadays, the park is very popular, and there are many other people running very early in the mornings who beat me to them, so I never find any duck eggs any more. Either that, or ducks have stopped laying eggs in the spring, which I doubt.

Next, my route heads upward and I go through the pavilion and the rose garden. This is really a big-time rose garden, and I never walk through the park without going through it. The other day I ran across a rose fancier there who'd come all the way from Chicago, and he said the "Double Delights" in this garden were better than he'd seen anywhere.

In the middle of the rose garden is a fountain that was the gift of another rich man, and during the summer it's generally full of little kids in their underwear. For a long time the Park Department tried to keep them out of it on the grounds that the water wasn't very clean, but lately I guess the Park Department doesn't care any more because nobody stops them. My dog always stops and drinks out of the fountain.

Once you get past the rose garden, you turn south and walk along the west edge of the park.

Along here are some great big mansions left over from the days when the park was a fancy golf course. One of them even has a bowling alley in the basement; they thought big in those days. The people in the mansions could sit on their front porch and watch the golfers in their plus-fours. Nowadays they can sit and watch the joggers, both men and women, in their striped, skin-tight jogging suits, and that's probably more fun than watching people in plus-fours.

And pretty soon you come to the tennis courts where there's always lots of action, people playing tennis, people sitting around watching and talking, dogs fighting and so forth.

From the tennis courts, you keep on going south, through a big grove of pine trees called (by me) The Black Forest, and then pretty soon you're back at the corner where you started, and we head on home.

So that's what it's like to walk around the park, but I haven't told you half of what we've seen over the years.

For one thing, the dog and I have been to lots and lots of weddings. If you want to get married in the rose garden, which is the favorite place in the park for weddings, you have to call the Park Department and make a date, that is, once you've decided on the girl and everything. But most every Saturday and Sunday during the spring and summer, there are weddings in the rose garden, with brides and lots of bridesmaids, and grooms in pink tuxedos or white tailcoats. Even though they've called the Park Department and made a date, still it is a public park, so my dog and I always stay for the rice-throwing, and the little kids in their underwear in the fountain keep right on screaming during the solemn vows. It's always great to go to a wedding.

But they don't do balloon ascensions after the weddings any more, and I don't know if that's because balloon ascensions are out as a feature of modern weddings, or because the Park Department won't let them do it any more. But we've seen several really thrilling balloon rides with the bride and groom floating away overhead flourishing champagne bottles, and the people cheering and the dogs barking and so forth.

The park is a lot busier than it used to be, so there aren't as many lovers in the park any more. But you have no idea how much love-making goes on in city parks on spring mornings, even really early in the morning. It's not exactly like Rome, where everybody seems to be making love in the parks any time of the day, but still, even as busy as it is now, our park gets quite a bit of one-on-one action. But it's nothing like it was in the old days when I could see almost anything on a spring morning as I was carrying home my duck eggs.

I started out as really the only jogger, but then slowly more people started, and now, of course, the joggers are there in droves. At first, it was men, and then I noticed more and more women. I used to count them and kind of keep score — for instance, there'd be ten men to two women. Then it got to be ten men to ten women. Nowadays it's lots more women than men, and that's a lot more fun for everybody. And the things they wear to go jogging are really something. In the summer, most of them don't wear anything at all, hardly. The macho young men are shirtless, and the women wear the shortest shorts imaginable. Lately I've noticed there's this big trend toward skin-tight striped jogging pants, and I can't imagine where they buy them, not in any store I go to.

Years ago I was jogging alone in the park on a dark wintry morning and I prevented a mugging. I was just jogging along and came upon a woman jogger who was starting to get mugged. I chased the mugger away and jogged after him really fast until he got in his car and drove off. The woman jogger caught up with me and gave me a great sweaty hug for saving her.

And not too long ago, a woman who lived across the street from the park was driving her car out of her driveway at night and the accelerator stuck, so she drove her car right straight into the park and hit a big tree and almost killed herself. My dog and I were there early the next morning, and we saw the car in the middle of the park, and the newspaper taking pictures and so on. My dog was in one of the pictures.

It used to be that every once in a while you'd hear about a rape in the park. Then all the neighbors would get uptight and keep calling the police and everything. I never saw anything like that, although I used to see streakers occasionally when that was a popular thing to do. And I used to see lots of people smoking marijuana, all sitting around together, looking a little depressed. But I don't see that any more either. The people in this park are just into health these days.

So, if you've reached the Golden Years and you're starting to become a "portly" and you're looking for something healthful that's interesting and cheap to do, and if you happen to live near a park and have a very old dog, try walking around the park every single day, counter-clockwise.

CHAPTER FOURTEEN

A Night Out
or
Appassionata

Getting ready for the recital

WHEN YOU'RE OLD ENOUGH TO RETIRE, and you finally have that gold watch, then, according to the retirement manuals, you and your wife will both start leading a new, demanding and dynamic life.

My wife started to lead her new dynamic life by taking piano lessons. She practices whenever she gets a chance, which means I have to start leading my new dynamic life some place else other than at our house.

But her new lifestyle has involved me in it because I not only listen to her practice, but I also go to her recitals.

She had her first recital the other day, and I haven't seen her so excited since the day we got married. We've gone to piano recitals for years when our children were taking piano lessons, and both my wife and I were fairly blase about it, and if the kid sounded good and didn't make a lot of mistakes, then we'd buy him a hamburger afterwards. But when my wife is the star of the afternoon, it's a different matter. I had to buy her two martinis and an expensive veal dish just to calm her down.

Anyway, the other benefit I get out of her new interest is that I get a big night out every once in a while to go and listen to these big-time traveling stars who come to town. The other day my wife announced that one was coming to put on a concert, and we were going. I was thrilled to hear about it. His name is Richard Goode, and he's a star on the concert circuit and plays Carnegie Hall and all that. He comes to our town about once every six weeks. He's working on playing all of Beethoven's Sonatas for us, of which there are 32 (thirty-two)! He's memorized them all, believe it or not. It'd be like memorizing all of Shakespeare, and then reciting a couple of different plays each night. Incidentally, in case anybody ever asks you, the first man who ever memorized all 32 of Beethoven's piano sonatas was a German named Arthur Schnabel who played them in 1927 in a series of four successive Sunday afternoons in Berlin. (They must have been LONG afternoons.) Anyway, by some stroke of luck I had missed his first two concerts, so he was up as far as Sonata Number 23 before I got in on the action. Actually, on the night I went, he played No. 3, No. 10, No. 12 and No. 6, apparently more or less at random, in addition to No. 23.

But number 23 is the real biggie; it's called "The Appassionata," and according to the program notes it's an "exceptionally explosive and compelling work."

"Sounds like it's got my name on it," I said to my wife. "I believe I knew that girl in high school."

"Try not to sleep through it," she said.

It turned out that we were going out to dinner before the concert, and we were going to take another music-loving couple with us, the Greers. Like my wife, Mr. Greer is a Beethoven aficionado, and like me, Mrs. Greer goes to the concerts with him in preference to staying home alone and watching reruns of "Three's Company." But both of them, like me, enjoy a couple of belts and a nice restaurant dinner before their Beethoven.

So we picked up the Greers and went downtown and had a couple of martinis before a really nice dinner. These days, the only thing the Golden Years crowd ever eats is fish and lettuce, so that's what we all ordered. I felt this was going to be the most exciting part of my night out, so I really enjoyed it. I wore one of my new custom-made shirts and my best suit, which was also new.

The Greers' seats are right in front of ours at the concert, and they had managed to get to the earlier concerts which I had missed, so Mrs. Greer brought along the program notes to read to us during dinner. She read aloud about The Appassionata during the soup course:

"The opening measures define musical dimensions as well as materials: a span of two octaves, doubled two octaves below; a time scale in relatively long units, alternating with short notes that imply the potential of more rapid movement; triad and diminished-seventh chord supporting the trill." There was lots more like this, and I began to think that maybe "Three's Company" might not have been such a bad choice after all. The more she read, the more I thought that maybe The Appassionata didn't sound like what I had in mind for my big night out. Anyway, the fish and lettuce dinner was good, and I enjoyed it a lot.

The concert hall was just packed.

"I guess a lot of people want to hear the principal motivic elements," I whispered to my wife.

"Wait till you hear the witty coda," she said.

Well, the first two numbers, that is, Sonata Number 3 and Sonata Number 14, went as well as could be expected. Mr. Goode, the out-of-town star, was really unusual to watch, because he hummed right along with his playing. It was very distracting at first, but pretty soon, even watching him as he sang and hummed and closed his eyes and blew out his cheeks and nodded and shook his head and smiled and frowned and talked to himself, even all that action got just a little old after awhile.

But then came The Appassionata, and Mr. Goode really knocked himself out on that one. I thought he was active during the first two numbers, but this one literally made him jump. I've never seen anybody work so hard at making music. He not only sang and hummed and blew out his cheeks and nodded his head and smiled and frowned and all those things, but he worked hard with his whole body and especially, of course, his arms and hands which were really pounding away, and he never made a single mistake, as far as I could see. It was fascinating, and I couldn't take my eyes off him.

To my amazement, Mr. Greer, the Beethoven-lover sitting in front of me, kind of nodded off during this frantic performance. I couldn't believe it. Here was the big moment of the evening, and he was missing it. I poked him gently, and he perked up a little, but then he went back to nodding.

For my own part, I was fascinated by the whole performance. It required my absolute complete attention and concentration. I couldn't possibly look away or try to focus on anything other than the music and Mr. Goode on the stage. When it was over, I was exhausted, and I suppose Mr. Goode was, too.

Later, going home in the car, we all talked about how thrilled we were by The Appassionata. I probably talked more about it than the others; my wife says I generally do. But then, I really was thrilled.

Mr. Greer allowed as how he had slipped away for just a few minutes. I didn't say anything, but I knew how long he'd been gone, and I knew he couldn't blame it on that little dab of fish and lettuce as having been too heavy.

Anyway, the very next week my wife tells me there's another piano player coming to town, and she doesn't want to miss a single one. So I'm to get another exciting night on the town! We invite another couple, not the Greers this time, and have another fish and lettuce dinner downtown.

This new pianist is named Kartsonis, and he hails from Cyprus, which is not a place particularly associated with piano prodigies in my mind. He's going to play some little-known numbers by Lizst. You and I both know that if the numbers are "little-known," then they probably aren't very good. Actually, even Lizst's well-known numbers probably aren't really that well known to me.

Anyway, Mr. Kartsonis has this great head of curly hair, and unlike Mr. Goode from the other night, he's young and slim. He announces when he sits down that the numbers he's going to play require a lot of concentration from the audience. This sends up a red flag for me. It was hard enough for me to concentrate on such a well-known old chestnut as the Appassionata the other night; I can't concentrate any harder than that.

And those Liszt numbers really were a bore; that's why they're little known. And what was worse, Mr. Kartsonis didn't goof around at all. I mean he didn't smile or laugh or frown or blow out his cheeks or hum or tap his foot or give us anything like the antics of Mr. Goode, which I'd really enjoyed. He just stared right straight ahead as if he were looking at the sheet music, which he wasn't doing, since he had the whole thing memorized.

I worked at it for a long time, and then I started to nod off, like my friend had done the other night. I stirred myself enough to applaud with everybody else at the end.

When we got home, I said to my wife, "Wow! What a great night out!"

She said, "When you reach the Golden Years, you're entitled to a new dynamic lifestyle. Hope you're enjoying it."

CHAPTER FIFTEEN

Hard of Hearing

IF YOU ARE RETIRING, or even thinking about it, you might as well get used to the fact that more and more people you know are getting deaf.

You notice this out on the golf course, for instance. You see four oldsters standing around on a putting green, shouting at each other, even though they're all right there together.

And even with all the advances in modern medicine, they haven't really been able to do much about it.

I know, because my mother was hard of hearing, and she had a hearing aid that worked just as well as President Reagan's used to do. Hers was bigger and bulkier, and she didn't try to hide it the way President Reagan did. In fact, she held it in her lap most of the time and sort of aimed it at the person she chose to listen to. It was a directional thing, and sometimes she'd hold it up toward you if she didn't want to miss anything.

The batteries in those days weren't nearly as good as they are today, and my mother was always conserving her batteries by turning her hearing aid off. It made a loud click when she turned it off. That meant she'd heard enough of whatever was going on around her. After that she'd just sit back and smile.

Sometimes, in the middle of an interesting conversation which she didn't want to miss, her batteries would get weak. She always carried spares in her pocketbook so she'd stop the conversation while she changed batteries. This required the use of a battery tester which she also carried with her, and the whole performance took a long time. Most of the other people had lost interest in that particular conversation before she arrived back on stream and brought the conversation right back to where it was when she checked out.

For more formal groups outside the family circle, she wore her hearing aid battery pack inside the front of her dress, where she could deftly, or so she thought, reach in and turn the machine on and off as the mood struck her. Many times I've seen her, while engaged in an apparently spirited conversation, reach inside her dress and turn her hearing aid off, click, thus signaling to everyone who knew her that the conversation was finished.

Changing batteries with the battery pack inside her dress was a little difficult, but she could do it. She'd reach inside her blouse and come up with two of these biggish batteries, sometimes surprising the other people who didn't know her.

Growing up in a household like that where the mother was hard of hearing has some advantages. I soon learned that she could read lips, even though she'd never really been taught to do it. At the dinner table I could say anything I wanted to and she wouldn't catch it if I just held my napkin up in front of my face.

Even though my mother was hard of hearing, I never dreamed that one day I, too, might grow to be that way. Of course, I'm not hard of hearing now at all, but certainly more and more people I know are.

My brother, for instance, is just deaf as a post. He can't hear thunder, even though he has an expensive hearing aid. But he's getting to be just like my mother — he frequently doesn't turn it on. I can have a long heart-to-heart conversation with him, and when it's all over I find he didn't have his hearing aid turned on. This is very irritating, and people who wear hearing aids should wear little signs that say, "Hearing Aid On," or if they choose, "Hearing Aid Off," so everyone will know where they stand. I think that when they were talking about Iran and the contras and all that, Mr. Reagan had his hearing aid turned off.

I know that people who wear hearing aids have a terrible time at big parties. That's because the hearing aid can't differentiate between the good conversations and all the bad noises that our regular ears tend to filter out, like other people's conversations and the sounds of glasses clinking everywhere and things like that. So the poor deaf person has to listen to the entire party, whether he wants to or not, and that soon grows tiring, so they either go on home or else turn their machine off, which is the equivalent of going on home.

As I say, as you get older, it seems everybody is getting deaf. Now, in addition to my brother, even my dog is getting deaf, and that's even more inconvenient for me, because the dog lives at my house. He won't come when I call him. He's not trying to be spiteful or anything, he just can't hear me. I can whistle and whistle, when the dog is right there under my nose, but he ignores me. If the burglars only knew that the giant, fierce-looking German Shepherd that lives at my house can't hear thunder, they'd feel a lot safer.

Now that I'm retired and hanging around the house a lot more than I used to, I find I'm talking to the dog a lot more than I ever did before. They say it's good for old people's self-esteem to have a dog to talk to, and I have always talked to mine a good deal, even before I was an old person. I give him my thoughts about the weather and make observations about the neighbors, things like that. I generally limit my conversation with him to things he knows something about, although occasionally I get into politics which is a foreign field for him.

But now that he's gotten pretty deaf, I find I have to holler at him, and our conversations have become even more awkward. My wife thinks it's nuts for me to be hollering at the dog all the time, but I think it'd be even nuttier for me to talk to him in my normal voice when I know he can't hear me.

Luckily, my wife hasn't started getting deaf yet and neither have I, but as our Golden Years progress, I'm sure hoping they make some kind of a new breakthrough in the hearing aid business.

— CHAPTER SIXTEEN —

Salvation Army

Lucy's rocker and the picnic table

ONCE YOU'RE COMFORTABLY AND HONORABLY RETIRED and settled into the snail-like pace of the Golden Years, then something is sure to come along and upset everything, like for instance in my case, my wife decided we should move.

It's true we've lived there almost forever; I can't remember when we didn't. And it's also true that we have far too much space and the house probably needs a new roof, and we can get a good price for it right now from some unsuspecting yuppie, and on and on like that, so I agree, very tentatively. Then, of course, we have to start taking steps to implement the decision.

That means starting, just starting, to get rid of the junk

we've accumulated in that house over the years. That's the first step toward moving, and it's not an easy one.

All our children were raised there, and they left behind in their various rooms all their childhood memorabilia and other junk they didn't want to take with them when they moved away. That's just part of it though. The other part is that during the time we've lived there, my wife's grandparents closed their house and died, my wife's parents closed their house and died, and my own parents did the same. So we have lots and lots of extra furniture and things like that which nobody, including us, wants.

It's one thing to say you don't want all this junk, and it's another thing to get rid of it.

The way we did was to start in the garage. In the past few years, as our house started to overflow with junk, we've been moving the worst items out to the garage. Old furniture, school desks, steamer trunks, step ladders, old porch rugs, you name it, everything ended up there as a spot of last resort. In addition, there were also a lot of garage items like old lawnmowers, plus two bicycles. The two bicycles belonged to our married daughter, and one day I ran across her stealthily squirreling away something else in that garage, and I asked her politely to remove her bicycles and anything else that belonged to her, so I could go about my assigned business of cleaning out the garage.

She said, "It's no problem. I'll just call the Salvation Army, and they'll come and pick them up."

"Wonderful," I said. "Let me know how it works out."

I forgot all about it for a couple of weeks, and then one afternoon she called and said, "The Salvation Army is coming tomorrow. Whatever it is you want to get rid of, now's your chance!"

My wife was thrilled. She started right away to make a list of additional items the Salvation Army could pick up on this trip. And during the cocktail hour that evening we started to assemble them in front of the garage. The Salvation Army won't come into your house to carry anything out, so you have to have it all outside and ready to go. Furthermore, they won't even drive their truck up your driveway, so they have to carry it down themselves, but that's their problem.

My wife and I had quite a lot of fun carrying things out of the basement and piling them in front of the garage. Chairs of various kinds, including two really bad-looking green velvet host and hostess chairs that she thought were really great-looking about fifteen years ago. We laughed and joked about them and had another drink. It was a lot of togetherness; the folks who move furniture together stay together.

After she got tired of doing that, she started looking around at the patio and the porch furniture.

"Might as well get rid of as much junk as we can in this one trip," she said. "Let's give them the picnic table."

"The picnic table?" I said. "Just because we're thinking about moving doesn't mean we won't have any more picnics."

"Well, we're going to Italy for a month next week, and after that we won't be able to have any more picnics this years, and when we get back from California in the spring, we'll be selling the house, so we won't have any more picnics then either, so let's just give the picnic table to some deserving clients of the Salvation Army. Once we get settled in our new place we can get a new picnic table if people have picnics there, which they probably don't do anyway."

Her logic seemed incontrovertible, so we added the picnic table and the picnic benches to the pile of Salvation Army stuff, in spite of the fact that I've always liked picnics, and that particular table carried a lot of nostalgia for me, memories of the kids falling off the benches backwards and so forth.

"And here's another item," she said. "Help me carry it over to the garage, and then we can go in and eat dinner."

This last item was one she found on the porch, a hand-made hickory rocker. The rocker had an interesting history, or at least it was interesting to me.

It had been given to us by our former next-door neighbor, an elderly lady named Lucy Durwood. Lucy was one of the few remaining relatives of another even more elderly lady who lived in a great big mansion not too far away, a lady named Mrs. Bernardin, whom Lucy called "cousin Sally."

When cousin Sally was getting so elderly she couldn't live in her big mansion any longer, she decided to have a giant garage sale and dispose of everything she owned. On the day before the sale, she called her cousin Lucy and asked her to come over and take anything she wanted. Well, Lucy Durwood already had a house full of junk, and being a very level-headed lady and also very elderly, she realized she didn't want any of her cousin Sally's garage sale junk. But she went over and went through Sally's house and came back and told my wife that Sally's chauffeur was bringing over the one thing she took out of Sally's house. It was an antique hand-made hickory rocker, and Lucy Durwood said she'd selected it because she thought my wife might want it.

By and by the chauffeur came and brought the chair.

"It was cousin Sally's favorite chair," Lucy said. "She used to sit in that chair on the front porch and watch the cars go by."

With an impeccable history like that, nobody could turn down a hand-made hickory rocker, one that Mrs. Bernardin sat in while watching the traffic. Anyway, the chauffeur put it on our porch, and from time to time somebody sat in it, although not very frequently, since we almost never use the porch any more. That was many years ago.

"It doesn't match any of the other porch furniture, it takes up a lot of room on the porch, we are definitely not going to take it with us when we move, and besides, those old ladies won't care what we've done with it, so let's just add it to the Salvation Army stuff," my wife said, as I was finishing my last cocktail.

"Anything to get on with dinner," I said. "Although it really is a shame to see Mrs. Bernardin's favorite antique hand-made hickory rocker going to the Salvation Army."

"Get used to it," my wife said.

When we were eating dinner, our daughter called to remind us that the Salvation Army was coming the next day.

"When are they coming?" my wife asked her.

"Sometime between noon and three-thirty," I heard my daughter say over the telephone.

"All right, I'll tell your father," my wife said, and hung up.

"I can't be here when the Salvation Army comes tomorrow," my wife said to me when the telephone conversation was over. "I already have a long list of things I have to do out of the house, including playing bridge all day at Betty's, so you'll have to handle the Salvation Army. And they'll be here sometime between noon and three-thirty. You'll just have to arrange your schedule to meet them. Make sure they take every single item."

"I think it is very inconsiderate of the Salvation Army, and extremely poor planning on their part, not to know any closer than that when they're going to be here," I said, finally realizing that this whole caper now hinged on my hanging around the house all the next afternoon.

"While you're waiting, why don't you start cleaning out the attic," my wife said.

"Let's see how this works before we go any further," I said.

Well, I spent the afternoon home alone, not cleaning out the attic, and the Salvation Army finally came about three-thirty, just at the very last minute.

The driver said he had orders to pick up two bicycles and two boxes of bric-a-brac.

"Two boxes of bric-a-brac?" I said. "I have a garage and a driveway full of furniture, and no bric-a-brac at all. Here, I'll just help you load this stuff." At this point, remembering my wife's admonition to get him to take everything, I certainly didn't want him to get away without taking my valuables with him.

So, slowly, very slowly, we carried things down to his truck which was getting crammed very full. As we carried more things down, the driver eyed every item more closely. And the very last items left on the driveway in front of the garage were the picnic table with its benches and the hickory rocker.

He looked those over very carefully.

"I can't take those things," he said, finally. "They're not good enough. They'd just go into the crusher."

I thought about telling him all about Mrs. Bernardin, and how that was her favorite antique porch chair, and I thought about telling him how I didn't want to get rid of the picnic table anyway, but I didn't. If he couldn't see the value in those things, that was his loss, I felt, his and the Salvation Army's.

Later on, when my wife came home, she was really disappointed that the picnic table was back on the patio where it always used to be, and the rocker was back on the porch. She said that if she'd been home she would have talked the Salvation Army man into taking those things, and I said if that's the way she felt, she ought to stay home more instead of gallivanting all over town all day. She said the next time we call the Salvation Army she'd be home, and I said I wouldn't be.

CHAPTER SEVENTEEN

The Importance of Living

Throwing away books my mother gave me

ONCE YOU'RE REALLY RETIRED and you've joined the ranks of the Golden Agers and you're comfortably settled for the rest of your life, then one of the first things you're going to have to do is move.

The house where you've lived for the past twenty-five years is too big or it's too small, or it's too close in, or too far out in the country, or it has too much lawn or it doesn't have any garden, or any number of other possible things is wrong with it, and your wife decides it's time to move, and eventually you end up agreeing with her.

At this point I'm not going to go into all the various possible traumas associated with this experience, just one of them.

And that one has to do with getting rid of things. In my case, my wife decided our house was too big. We should move into a smaller place, a condo, where we'd be free to come and go when we want to, and where we'd be free from thieves that break in and steal, and where I'd be free from the necessity of having to cut the grass.

Fine.

But there's a catch to it. And the catch is, you have to get rid of lots of things, especially lots of books.

Over the years we have accumulated a lot of books. A book is a wonderful gift; it shows thought, it makes a nice-size present, it's easy to wrap, the price is right, and it promises hours of entertainment to the recipient. So we've given each other lots of books over the years, and our children have given us books, and our friends have given us books, and we still have them all.

Besides that, at one time in our earnest young married life we belonged to the Book-of-the-Month-Club, and before we could realize what was happening and staunch the flow, we found ourselves absolutely swamped with nice-looking hardback books, many of which never got read but which always ended up on the shelves.

In addition, our two sets of parents were book-savers before us. They had run across this problem themselves when they closed their houses, and rather than throw their own books away, they offered them to us and, foolishly, we took them. Over the years we've been reluctant to throw away their books, thinking that if my father, for instance, thought a particular book was worth saving, probably we ought to hang onto it and maybe someday read it. Little did we suspect that he'd probably never read it either.

Anyway, the sum total of all this is that we have an awful

lot of books, and we're moving into a smaller place, and we're going to have to get rid of most of them.

The way we get rid of our books is to give them to a convenient thrift shop called the "Nearly New." That's where we take everything we're not going to move to our new place, and they're very pleased to get our stuff. I suspect they make some money out of it and their customers are pleased with it, and some small profit accrues to the symphony or whatever the organization is that benefits from their activities. It's all very worthwhile and satisfying.

The other day my wife announced that she was going to make a run to the Nearly New. She had almost filled the car with an assortment of really great items that would be welcome there.

She said, "I have room in the car for a couple of big boxes of heavy books. Since it's raining and you don't have anything to do, and since I have a couple of big boxes here, why don't you go upstairs and fill them with books we don't want, and I'll take them to the Nearly New."

With that, she gave me these two really big boxes and stepped back out of the way so I could go up to the third floor where we keep the old books. When we moved into that house twenty-five years ago, I carried a lot of things, including a lot of books, from the third floor of our old house to the third floor of the new house. Most of them we've never looked at since. It does seem to be a good rule that if you've had something in your house for twenty-five years and you've never looked at it, then there's a reasonably good chance you don't need it.

Anyway, I took the two boxes and went up to the third floor. Our third floor has three fairly big dormer windows, and one of these dormers has been used as a catch-all for many years and contains, among a lot of other things, two giant old-fashioned glass-front bookcases covered with dust. I decided to start with the bottom shelf of the furthest bookcase, and in order to do that I had to crawl into the dormer space on my hands and knees because the dormer is so full of other things, and then I had to lie on my side and pull up the glass door of the bookcase in order to pull out the books. From that position I could throw each individual book out into the room to be put into the boxes later.

Everything went well for a while. I had happened upon some shelves from our Book-of-the-Month-Club period, and there's no question but what the January 1963 alternate choice of the Book-of-the-Month Club is something you don't have to keep at hand when you move into a smaller place. So the Nearly New was getting lots of great-looking books. I even discovered, and remembered, that there'd been some confusion for a few years with the Book-of-the-Month Club, and they'd sent us two copies of their selections, both of which we'd dutifully kept on hand.

But then it started to get a little harder. I ran across several shelves of books that had come from my parents' house. I didn't feel quite so cavalier about throwing these away, particularly books which my parents had given to me as a youth.

"Robinson Crusoe" was inscribed, "To George, from Mother, Christmas 1939." But with a stiff upper lip I threw it out into the middle of the room along with all the others. I was awfully uncomfortable lying on the floor in that cramped position, and the discomfort was helping me make quick decisions.

This went on a long time, and the pile of throwaways was growing while my arm was going to sleep.

I paused for a few minutes when I came across "The Importance of Living," by Lin Yutang. This one was inscribed, "To George, from Mother, Christmas 1944." It's the original self-help book but, applying my rule about not needing things you hadn't even known you owned for the past twenty-five years, I manfully threw it into the discard pile.

Next came a shelf of college textbooks, both mine and my wife's. If there's anything you don't need at our advanced age, it's a third-year Latin or a Differential Calculus or An Introduction to Ethics. Some of those books were big heavy ones, and I felt really grateful that I wouldn't need to move them again after today.

I hadn't realized it, but while I was lying cramped on the floor in the dormer space throwing books out into the room, my wife had arrived on the third floor and was sitting in the middle of the room examining every one of my throwaway selections. She had divided them into two piles.

"What are you doing?" I asked her when I had finally crawled out from the dormer and was able to stand upright.

"This pile we're throwing away, and these we're keeping," she said. I looked through her pile of keepers.

"You've got to be kidding," I said. "Who wants 'The History of Architecture 1900-1930'?"

"I do," she said. "I loved that course."

"But it's a big heavy book, and you'll never look at it again as long as you live," I said.

"I want to keep it," she said.

Then I looked at her throwaway pile. And right on top was "The Importance of Living" by Lin Yutang, a gift from my mother.

"Well, if you're keeping "The History of Architecture, 1900-1930," then we're certainly keeping 'The Importance of Living' by Lin Yutang. Look, my mother gave it to me thinking it might do me some good, and she inscribed it to me."

Somewhat coolly, I thought, my wife said, "What's it about? Have you read it?"

"No, but I guess my mother did."

"If your mother gave it to you in 1944 and you've never read it, then I guess we can give it away," she said. "At least I have read "The History of Architecture, 1900-1930."

"When my mother gave that book to me, I was in the Navy in the Pacific Ocean learning about the importance of trying to stay alive. That's why I never got around to reading it."

"Would you read it now if we kept it?" she said.

"Not right now, I'm in the middle of something else. But I'll put it on my list," I said.

"Look," she said. "Here's the *Readers' Digest* condensed version: 'The Importance of Living' by Lin Yutang. Abridged by experts. We can keep that one and throw the big one away."

"If we don't want the real thing, then we don't want a shorter version of it," I said.

Later, I carried two big boxes of books down to the car, and my wife put a lot of others back on the shelf. I told myself those are two big heavy boxes I won't have to find room for at our new place. And later that night I thought to myself that some worthy customer of the Nearly New would probably get a big kick out of reading "The Importance of Living" by Lin Yutang.

Probably do somebody a lot of good.

CHAPTER EIGHTEEN

Wrinkle City

Patrolling the project

ONCE YOU'RE FINALLY RETIRED, and you've got your gold watch, and you've heard all the speeches and congratulations, then you can settle down to the really stressful part of your life. The kids are gone, leaving nothing but their cast-off clothing which they won't let you throw away, and their old text books, and their year books, plus their empty bedrooms which somebody has to keep dusted.

Before long, just as you're getting used to your new relaxed lifestyle, your wife decides to sell the house and move. In my case I found out about it when I discovered my wife had been having afternoon assignations with a real estate agent, looking at expensive condos.

Once she'd taken that first tentative step, once she'd looked at her first condo, the die was cast, and that was before I knew anything about it. Next thing I knew, she started selling some of the furniture out of our house, giving some to the Salvation Army, and shipping some to the kids who live 700 miles away.

She located just the right condo in an amazingly short time. It was in an overpriced little area in the southern part of town where a number of our older acquaintances had settled after selling their big houses. Everybody, including me, laughingly called it "Wrinkle City."

"We're too young to move to Wrinkle City," I said.

"You'd better stop calling it that," my wife said. "Nobody who lives there calls it that."

"I don't live there," I replied, getting a little alarmed.

"I think you're probably going to," she said, prophetically.

And so that's how I moved to Wrinkle City, and I still slip and call it that occasionally.

Wrinkle City "proper" is really named Chapman Downs and used to be the farm of a rich merchant who raised race horses. Of course, the barns and all that are long gone, and now there's just all these fancy condos and lovely grass and trees and lots of green space and sprinklers. The whole thing is surrounded by a high wrought iron fence, and you push a button in your car to open the gate.

The part of Wrinkle City where my wife found the condo of her dreams is called Jefferson Court. This is thirty condos in a "Williamsburg-like setting" surrounding a swimming pool (one like they used to have in Williamsburg).

What it really is, on first glance, is garage doors. Identical white garage doors. The people who live in these thirty condos come and go in their cars, of course. And when they come, they drive into the garage, and that's the last you ever see of them until they drive away again.

When I first moved there, I'd be standing outside my condo talking to my dog, for instance, and one of my neighbors would drive in, and what I thought they were doing was waving to me. So I waved back with a big smile, even though I didn't know them. Later I discovered they weren't waving to me at all, they were simply reaching up to touch the button on their visor that would raise their garage door, and it looked like they were waving. They probably wondered why that stranger was standing there smiling and waving.

When I first told my friends I was moving to Wrinkle City, everybody said, "Oh, there's so much partying goes on out there, and people lead such a fast life, you'll have to be careful." Well, what a laugh. The fast life in Wrinkle City consists of a cocktail party now and then. It always starts at 5:30 and you're home by 8:30, with dinner over and nothing to do until the ten o'clock news.

I haven't lived there very long, but I've already gotten to know some of the other people. This is unusual, because some people have lived there for years and still don't know anybody.

But the reason I've met some people is because I walk my dog around the project.

This is a very elderly female German Shepherd that was left temporarily in my care by one of my children who got married and moved 700 miles away seven years ago, and she walks very slowly. I almost have to drag her along sometimes and, of course, this always gets a smile and a remark out of anybody who happens to see us, which isn't really very often. A friendly old dog is a great ice-breaker.

But there's a downside to it, too. People in Wrinkle City don't like even friendly old dogs to use their carefully manicured expensive green space for anything except gazing at. So the trick is, I must hustle my old dog out the gates of the project as quickly as I can. After being outside the gates long enough, then we can come strolling leisurely home again, just gazing at the lawns with impunity, and saying hello to what few people we happen to catch outside their garage doors.

Very few people in Wrinkle City have dogs. That's because of the old saying about when the children leave home and the dog dies, then you can think about moving into a condo. All these people waited until their dog died before they moved. So I'm unusual to have moved my old dog with me, and even more unusual than that, I also brought a cat, which was also left in my care temporarily when another one of my children left home and moved 700 miles away five years ago. My dog and my cat sit on my patio watching life go (slowly) by, and they make my patio completely outstanding just by their presence. Thus, within a short period of time, my wife and I were, a little ominously, known around the neighborhood as "the people who have a dog and a cat."

I haven't heard any complaints yet, and that's because I hustle the old dog outside the gates as fast as she'll move whenever we go outside.

The kitty presents an additional problem. Sometimes I leave the kitty outside all night to patrol the project and keep a sharp watch out for mice or other undesirable aliens. Not long ago I did this, and when I went outside in the morning to greet the dawn, I found the kitty had caught, eaten and regurgitated a largish animal, by the kitty's standards, possibly a baby rabbit or a ground squirrel. And the act had taken place on my neighbor's patio.

There was fur all over, and the two wee little uneaten feet, and a portion of the head, plus, well, I won't go into the details, but obviously I had to do something about it before the neighbors woke up and went outside to get their morning paper.

So I quietly cleaned up the mess while cursing the kitty under my breath, and I managed to avoid any possible finger-pointing. But who knows when something like that might happen again and I couldn't get to it fast enough? That'd be the end of the kitty's good reputation in Jefferson Court. Besides my animals, one of the other things that makes my wife and me outstanding around the neighborhood is that we actually use the swimming pool. Most people think the swimming pool, like the green areas, is just for gazing at.

The reason nobody uses the pool is really simple. Everybody who lives there is probably between 55 and 85, and one thing everybody between 55 and 85 shares is bad skin. If you're going to the dermatologist once a month to have those cancery little bumps painfully and expensively removed, you're certainly not going to lounge around the swimming pool in the blazing sun any more. But my wife and I aren't quite as bad skin-wise as some of the others, I guess, and we sometimes run over to the pool and hop in, hoping the sun stays behind a cloud while we're there. And sometimes we take a cocktail there after the sun goes down. Nobody else does this because it's too much trouble; the pool is too far from the ice and mix.

We bought one of the smaller condos at Jefferson Court. It seems plenty big to me, and it seemed just what the doctor ordered at the time, for my wife, too. But now that she's lived there a few months, she's beginning to think maybe it's not big enough, so she's looking around. She likes Jefferson Court all right, and would like to stay there, but now that she's got the hang of moving, we just might be moving to the other side of the Williamsburg-style swimming pool any day, to a different condo of her dreams.

CHAPTER NINETEEN

The First Annual Wrinkle City Triathlon

WHEN YOU'RE OLD ENOUGH to retire early and your wife has talked you into selling the old house and moving into a condo, and the kids have all moved 700 or more miles away, then you start living an entirely new and different life. You're a new person. For one thing, you're a fatter and a lazier person. When you were young and working hard, the battle for the almighty dollar kept you reasonably slim, as well as tense and stressed out. Now that you've retired, and you've become a full-time consumer instead of a producer, you're still tense and stressed out, but no longer slim.

And, of course, if you're like me and you move into an upscale, over-priced condominium development where they have a full-time crew of perfectly developed young athletes who cut the grass and pick up all the gum wrappers, then, of course, you don't have any way at all to keep your own body from turning into pure flab. Before I moved to this condo development which I will call Wrinkle City, I had my own house and my own lawn, and I sometimes cut the grass and I always picked up the gum wrappers and the discarded beer bottles myself. That avenue of athletic endeavor has been closed to me now that the grounds crew around here is paid to do it. (And paid a lot, I might add.)

So the other day I decided to get my body back in shape.

"I'm going to enter the Wrinkle City Triathlon," I told my wife.

"When's it going to be?" she answered, a little sarcastically. "I want to be sure and get a good seat."

"I'll hold the Triathlon as soon as I get the necessary equipment," I said. "You have to have the proper equipment; it's not to be entered into carelessly."

The first part of any triathlon is running, or in the case of the W.C. Triathlon, a little light jogging mixed with a little brisk walking. So the first item of equipment needed is shoes.

And buying new running (or walking) shoes is an experience fraught with difficulty.

You don't buy them from a regular shoe salesman whom you know at a regular shoe store like where I buy my usual Frankensteins. Instead, you go to one of these sport shoe emporiums in a gigantic mall where young men who don't know you sell athletic shoes. And one of the difficulties about it is that you don't know what you want.

In the old days you could have asked for tennis shoes, or sneakers. You could still, but you'd be getting the wrong thing.

The shoes you want look a little like old-fashioned tennis shoes, but there's a world of difference. I just don't happen to know what it is.

"Do you want running shoes, sir?" That's the voice of the young man who works there.

"Well, I don't do a whole lot of running," I say. "Maybe just shoes to walk kind of fast in."

"Were you thinking of Reeboks, Adidas, Nikes, or Spiders?" he asks.

To tell the truth, I hadn't known enough to be thinking of any brand name, so I play it safe.

"Which do you recommend?"

And so, slowly and carefully, he leads me step by step to what is probably the most expensive pair of shoes in the store. I end up with a pair of high-top Reeboks. I chose them because I happened to remember that my son-in-law had just bought a new pair of high-top Reeboks. If he can afford them, so can I!

Now that I'm outfitted in shoes, I can start working out in preparation for the triathlon. I walk every day, very religiously. One of the features of my new shoes is that they're high-tops, and it takes a really big effort to lace them up. I mean, leaning over that long every time you put on your shoes is almost as good for you as the walk itself.

The second part of the triathlon is the bicycle ride. And once again, the equipment is important; you have to have a bicycle.

So I venture out again to the nearest gigantic mall where there's a bicycle store. And I'm really lucky to run into an extremely understanding and knowledgeable young lady named Wanda who's selling the bicycles.

Instead of asking me what kind of a bicycle I want, she realizes I probably don't know, so she tells me.

"You probably want a mountain bike instead of a road bike. Isn't that right?" That's what I call a salesperson! Of course,

I want a mountain bike instead of a road bike! I would have got around to that eventually, but she helped me a lot.

Actually, I didn't know what a mountain bike was until I met up with Wanda. In fact, it sounded a little strenuous.

A mountain bike is heavier than a road bike and sturdier, with bigger tires, and handlebars that let you sit up straighter. The other one, the road bike, is the one that you ride in the fetal position that looks so dreadfully uncomfortable. Never mind that the mountain bike is a little more expensive; Wanda assures me that's the one I want.

But even the mountain bike has several modern conveniences which I'm not familiar with, such as a ten-speed gear box and hand brakes. I ride it around the parking lot near the store, and Wanda shows me how to shift and tells me I'll catch onto the new things very quickly.

My wife had driven me to the shopping mall, and when she saw that my bike was ready to go, she went her way, leaving me to ride my new bicycle home. It wasn't much of a trip, just a couple of miles, but it was thrilling for me, dodging the traffic, having the cars honk at me, almost causing a wreck, forgetting for a moment how to use the hand brakes, and then discovering I was in the wrong gear the whole time. I did make it home, however, and I realized I would have to practice a good long time before entering the triathlon.

And so I did. I rode my new bicycle religiously every day for a little while around the swimming pool at Wrinkle City, and I learned how to use the brakes and the gearshift, and how to sit a little less uncomfortably on the hard, pointed seat. So, after several weeks of this warm-up, I decided I was ready.

I had mapped out a course for the Wrinkle City Triathlon and invited several of my acquaintances to enter with me. However, when the day actually came, they were all out at the club playing gin rummy, so I was the only one to enter the big event.

By this time I was old friends with my new high-top

Reeboks. By the time I get them laced up, I feel I've already had my exercise. But they stood up perfectly during the running portion of the event. To take just the teensiest short-cut, I cut across the parking lot at the nearby shopping center, then came the long straightaway to the park, and then once around the park. Then back home via the different, less hilly route, and the whole running (walking) part of the triathlon was behind me.

I immediately hopped on my bicycle for the riding portion, and I was off! The bicycle course is entirely different from the running course, naturally, and it is, if possible, even less hilly, although a lot longer. And it necessarily is on some pretty high-traffic streets because where I live can hardly be classified as "rural." Anyway, I'm glad to report that I didn't get hit by a car or cause an accident of any kind.

I did think it was a little odd that so many people honked and waved at me. I've lived in this town all my life, so I know a lot of people, but I don't know THAT many people. I finally decided that a lot of total strangers were honking and smiling and waving at me, and I couldn't help but wonder what was so funny. It was something about me wobbling along on that busy street on my new mountain bike, but they didn't know I was riding in the triathlon. They might have thought that was REALLY funny!

Anyway, when I finally made it back home after the cycling portion, I stripped off my sweaty cycling costume and into my swim trunks and headed for the pool.

Naturally there was nobody else in the pool. Nobody uses the pool at Wrinkle City except my wife and me; it's mainly just for looking at. But there I was, bravely doing my laps, and when I finished, I found myself standing comfortably relaxed in the warm, waist-deep water, with my wife efficiently handing me an ice-cold gin and tonic. Most triathlons don't end up that way, but I recommend it.

"How dull it is to pause, to make an end, to rust

unburnished, not to shine in use, as though to breathe were life," I recited, quite appropriately, I thought.

"Dinner will be ready in about fifteen minutes," my wife said. "Can you make it out of the pool?"

"Of course," I said. "But you know, all that walking hurts my knee, and riding that bicycle really gets to my back."

CHAPTER TWENTY

The Fast Life at Wrinkle City

ONCE YOU'RE RETIRED and you've sold your house and moved into a condo in a development like Wrinkle City where you and most of the other people are between the ages of 55 and 85, then you need new challenges. You've spent your entire adult life overcoming challenges in business; now the only challenges you have to face are close to home.

And moving to a place like Wrinkle City presents a lot of them. W.C. isn't exactly a retirement community, but then there aren't any kids there either. For one thing, it's got a bad name among young people; I mean, I didn't think I myself would ever be old enough to move to Wrinkle City until my wife explained it to me. But the real reason young people don't live there is because it's too expensive. Actually, it's too expensive for me, and probably for a lot of the other people, too, but what the hell.

One of the big challenges about moving to a place like that is getting to know somebody else who lives there. Where I live, it's just all garage doors — Garage Door City. People come and go in their cars, of course, and when they come home, they push a button in their car and the garage door goes up and they drive into their garage, and that's the last you ever see of them until they drive out again sometime to-morrow or next week.

When I first moved there, I used to stand outside my house on the driveway, waiting to say hello to somebody else who might be outside on the driveway. But nobody ever stepped outside his house. I waited for my neighbor to step outside and pick up his newspaper until I found out he was out of town and wasn't going to pick up the paper at all.

Nobody bakes an apple pie and brings it over to your house on the day you move in. In fact, nobody ever bakes apple pies at all at Wrinkle City, because all anybody ever eats any more is just fish and lettuce, and besides, all the ladies gave up baking long before they moved here.

And when you move in, nobody is sitting on their front porch swing watching the movers, like they used to do in the Good Old Days. In fact, when we moved in, I happened to catch one of my neighbors as she was pulling into her garage, and I introduced myself to her and told her we were moving into where the Swansons used to live.

She said, "The Swansons? Have they moved out?" Well, they'd been gone more than six months, but the next-door neighbor hadn't noticed. That's the kind of old-fashioned friendly atmosphere you have at Wrinkle City.

The condo we bought is one of the smaller ones in the whole place. As it is, we have four and a half baths and certainly don't need any more. But our place is in a building with five other condos. It's a six-plex, if there is such a thing, a "Williamsburg-style six-plex." We're in Unit No. 2 of this particular building.

It so happened that we knew, not very well, but we did know before we moved in, the couple who live in Unit No. 1. They're about our age, their children are grown and gone, she's an amateur painter and he plays golf a lot — a pretty typical outfit for Wrinkle City.

But we didn't know anybody else in our building, our six-plex.

So, after a few months of not knowing anybody, I said to my wife, "Let's have a party for our Roofmates." And so, eventually, we did.

Out in Wrinkle City, the management thoughtfully publishes a directory, so you know the names of everybody and where they live, also the wife's maiden name and other intimate details, even though you don't know them personally. So we knew that in Unit No. 3, next to us, there was a single lady; in Unit No. 4, a doctor and his wife; in Unit No. 5, a lawyer and his wife; and in Unit No. 6, another single lady. That was the lot of our Roofmates. And the way you invite them to a party is you drop the invitation into their mailbox, which we did.

Well, eventually the appointed day came, and we met our Roofmates. The first person to arrive was the single lady from No. 3, next door. She is a widow, approximately 75 years of age, and she had lived in her condo for fifteen years, but she had never been in ours before and she was interested in looking around and she said it was very nice, and she'd have a Scotch and water, not too much water.

Next came the lawyer and his wife from No. 5. They're

about our age, had lived in W.C. a long time, and also had never been in our house before. Apparently the people who lived in our place weren't very friendly. The lawyer took a martini, and his wife took a Scotch, not too much water.

Then the doctor and his wife from No. 4 arrived, along with the single lady from No. 6. They had never met officially, so they introduced themselves to each other on our doorstep. Can you believe it? I mean, living two doors away for ten years!

The No. 6 lady was somewhere between a greying 75 and a spry 80. She allowed as how she'd have a little bourbon with water, not too much water. The doctor, it turned out, is a plastic surgeon, and his wife is a travel agent. They both settled for Scotch. The couple from No. 1, the golf player and the lady artist, had been close friends of the travel agent in college, but they didn't realize it until they met her at our party.

Well, I want to tell you, everybody had a wonderful time! These people, most of whom had never met before, really hit it off. The lawyer and his wife from No. 5 were really world-class travelers. I mean, they have been to Moscow four times since 1979, and to most any other place you could mention. And, of course, the travel agent wife of the plastic surgeon really talked their arm off. She had just gotten back herself, from the southern lake country of Chile, which is one place the lawyer and his wife had not been, but they were thinking about it. (They have subsequently left for Chile.)

And the lady from Unit No. 3 has this peek-a-poo puppy, and she was really wanting to tell us all about it, and yes, she'd have another Scotch. And the other single lady (No. 6) had been wanting to meet the plastic surgeon because her grandson was thinking of going to medical school, and is business as good for plastic surgeons as everybody says it is? And, yes, she'd have another bourbon, not too much water, please.

And so it went for a good long time, with everybody really getting in there and mixing it up. The party was over much too soon as far as most everybody was concerned, although we'd told them in advance there'd be no food. Everybody went home to their own luxury condo and fixed dinner, probably fish and lettuce. But before they all left, several of the roofmates said we'd have to do this again, and it was a good idea, and a real first!

We haven't received an invitation for the next Roofmates party yet, but I'm sure we will.